PRAISE FOR CARA-JULIE KATHER

A deeply personal yet universal work of poetry that captures the feeling of grieving a loved one with an insurmountable beauty.

— NORA WUNDERWALD, AUTHOR OF
ON&OFF

Vitality and love are growing and blooming through every line. I cried a lot while reading—out of gratitude for the chance to live and love.

— SASKIA KÜHN, WRITING COACH AND
POETRY PEDAGOGUE

Kather's collection is stillness, an embodiment of quietude. It's a lesson and a dream and not a dream all at once. These poems take the amorphous nature of being present and paint a picture of presence that is palpable. It's a book that asks questions like, "I wonder if there is a specific logic to herbs?" One has to be slowed down to find this query amongst the leaves on the window or the rain in the air or the stillness of a tree next to the stillness of another person. There is a lesson in these poems about sitting and reading and writing and being with the self, the you, and opening the heart into a blossom of quiet.

— MATTHEW LIPPMAN, AUTHOR OF *WE
ARE ALL SLEEPING WITH OUR
SNEAKERS ON*

there are ginkgo leaves on the window is a "slow pirouette" into those relationships—beyond time and human boundaries—that give us our names. Cara-Julie Kather has the rare ability to capture that moment when grief turns into gratitude, and it's a gift to the reader.

— DR. CHIARA STEFANONI, FEMINIST PHILOSOPHER

A tender homage to live and the persistence of love beyond death.

— HELENA GERWIN, CO-FOUNDER OF FEMINIST BOOK CAFÉ "KAPITEL DREI"

Cara-Julie's writing "tastes" like a freshly brewed lavender tea: warm, unique, tender and grounding. The most customary gestures and movements become so precious in her poetry that one feels the urge to follow her in that. Her meticulous and loving observations reveal the naturalness and quality of her writing. I am reminded of the beauty of mourning, of remembering and nurturing the ancestral bond. It is obvious that she has no other choice but to write. And it is obvious that this fantastic book that is so genuine, yet complex and versatile in its form, must be read!

— PALOMA NANA, MUSICIAN AND INDEPENDENT RESEARCHER

THERE ARE GINKGO LEAVES ON THE WINDOW

LETTERS TO MY DECEASED GRANDMOTHER

CARA-JULIE KATHER

Fuente Fountain Books

Published by Fuente Fountain Books

1631 NE Broadway Street #737, Portland, Oregon 97232

www.fuentefountainbooks.com

Editor: Michael Favala Goldman

Author: Kather, Cara-Julie (1999), Germany

Title: *there are ginkgo leaves on the window: letters to my deceased grandmother*

ISBN-10 0-9843756-3-5 (pbk : alk. paper)

ISBN-13 978-0-9843756-3-9

ebook ISBN 979-8-9912634-0-5

1. Literature -Grief -Women -Letters -Memoir -Poetry -Metaphysical ancestor love.

2. Title.

First edition, printed in the United States of America, 2024

Cover art by Lynette Yetter, based on a photograph by Cara-Julie Kather

For my grandmother.

Thank you for writing with me.

CONTENTS

YOU

This might be the first time I inhabit a house all by myself for longer than just a few hours.

I make myself dinner. The simpleness of my plans makes me feel at ease. I am making dinner.

Then I will sit down and eat. Then I will study the house.

After the eating I sit. I become more still than I was for quite some time.

I can feel you here, Grandma. You slow me down. You take me in your arms.

Can I write a book with you please?

I know this might be harder to do now that your human shapes have left this earth.

But did you not leave all these things that make a book?

Did you not put all these a's in my pinky finger? And all these exclamation marks in my stomach?

I sometimes feel like there are so many books inside of me. You must have put some of them there, didn't you?

I think we should write the book in English. For I have never done that, and I want to know how it tastes.

I saw you today when I was looking at the cap Grandpa wore. Is that strange? Maybe not.

He misses you a lot. He wishes you visited his dreams more often. But maybe you are scared.

He looks very beautiful, you know.

We sit a lot.

He seems to study all your days and nights. He seems to move through all your decades of togetherness.

He builds all these futures and pasts.

He makes the most beautiful logic.

For example, he bought a Christmas tree and he told me: Because it is only me this Christmas, the tree is half the size to the years before.

He told me he only decided late to get a tree. There were only a few left and he walked straight up to the small one, had it wrapped, and drove it home.

It was quick because it was the logical tree.

We put the tree up together. Moving through all the boxes of decoration that had your handwritten labels on them.

Thank you for writing with me.

I would miss you so much, were we not writing this book.

But we are. We are writing the book.

What is it you want to write about?

It could be lots of things.

But please let us write.

You must be awfully alive for a dead person. Then again you have always been particularly alive.

Alive in modes very much your own.

I love you a lot.

I am afraid this sentence is too cliché for our book. But I want it there.

Can we write a book where we can put anything in there, please?

Can I ask you questions in our book?

You can ask me questions too if you'd like to.

We can also put names in our book. I think.

I am afraid of stopping to write.

I need this book to exist. I need to write it with you.

How can I do that?

Can you help me?

I love you.

There it is again.

I love clichés sometimes. I like the knowability, the comfort.

I want to be warm.

Can I take you in my arms please?

I think I have an idea for our book.

It might be an important one. But I don't know yet.

Can I tell you?

Maybe we can put their names as chapters.

Do you think we can write our book?

Do you think we can do it holding hands?

I love holding hands so dearly.

You put a 'z' on my tongue. Its taste reminds me of a lemon. Only it is much sweeter.

Thank you for the book.

LEO

On one of the first days he spent alone in the house, I asked him how it felt to be alone.

I was not alone, I was working, I was reading, he said.

My heart gave a little ache.

He never seems to be alone when studying.

Is it because you are there then?

Is it because studying is what you did together?

Is this why I am not alone right now?

I believe he makes his life through all the kinds and modes of study.

I already told you he studied your Christmas trees. Then he made an entire Christmas tree logic all by himself.

He studied your mornings too.

He told me.

He kept the mornings.

I remember how I sometimes stumbled into your mornings when we were living together.

Do you remember how we lived together?

Do you think making a book is a way of living together?

I would love that a lot.

He would too.

Do you know I gifted him a telescope for Christmas?

And a heavy book with thousands of pictures of the universe?

A few days after Christmas I called him to see if he wanted to go for a walk before having lunch.

His voice on the phone was hushed and he was quick to hang up.

I am in the middle of a project, he said, can you just come over?

When I arrived, I asked about his project.

He had studied the book. He had studied the telescope. He had studied the universe.

Did you hear that? He studies the universe!

He always did. I merely gifted him some new equipment.

Tomorrow he will come and pick me up.

This reminds me of when I was a child.

I wonder if there will still be gingko leaves in front of the house tomorrow.

There were a lot of them a few months back.

I picked some of them up.

I made a small collection of gingko leaves for him because I thought: That might be a good way to love him since gingko leaves were your favorite leaves.

I had never really noticed just how many gingko shaped items you had collected throughout the house!

The drawing of the gingko leaf in the hallway started greeting me only after you were gone.

But it does so very warmly now. I'm glad.

Your gingko shaped earrings are with me now.

I only wore them once so far. I am afraid of losing them.

When I saw all the gingko leaves in the driveway that day, I tried to memorize them all.

And I tried to love them all.

And I wonder if that's maybe the same thing.

Tomorrow, I will give him a hug and you will be there.

I am afraid I need to go to bed now.

I don't want to.

I am scared our book might disappear.

Can our book still be there when I wake up?

Can you promise me?

You promise me.

And I kiss you goodnight.

YOU

Hello. You.

I am in bed now, but I want to keep writing.

When I was still sitting downstairs, I drank tea made from thyme.

I have never drunken that before. This is what our writing tastes like to me now. Like thyme.

What happens when you mix thyme with ginkgo?

It seems it must create the most magical drink.

Or maybe the mixture would even amount to a small creature.

It seems likely that it would.

I wonder if there is a specific logic to herbs.

Are there any herbs where you are at?

Do you have a garden you can grow your favorite things in?

Did you know you are a writer?

I think a lot of people might not have told you because they assumed you knew.

This seems like another reason why it is good that we are making a book now.

Making a book can really make you know you are a writer.

Or at least I really hope it will.

My shoulders ache.

I think I might have a very weird posture.

Is that something I got from you?

I don't like that I need to go to sleep.

I wish I could at least kiss the ginkgo earrings goodnight before going to sleep.

But I can kiss you goodnight, I hope.

I might have a small story that can kiss you goodnight.

When I was still downstairs in the kitchen, I did a very slow pirouette.

I never have done a pirouette this slow.

I tried to do an even slower one on my other leg.

It worked.

Then I thought that maybe I can pirouette my way into sleep.

I will try that now.

I promise.

Sleep tight.

I love you.

I wonder if I can dream of ginkgoes.

Yes. I promised.

I promise.

I will tell you the story of my sleep tomorrow when we continue making our book.

I promise.

CHRISTINE

I did not like going to sleep yesterday. I wanted to keep writing.

I was scared our book might disappear while I was asleep.

But I see now that our book is still here. It still exists.

Do you still want to make the book?

I'm glad.

We need to have a chapter with her name, don't we?

Do you know I wear her ring every day?

I always put it on to write, even if I don't otherwise get dressed that day.

I remember a few years back you told me stories about her over the phone.

I had finally dared to ask for her stories. I had been wanting to do that since I was a child.

But I was afraid to make you sad.

On the phone that day you did not seem sad.

Were you sad?

You told me that she once poured water on the floor because she thought it was on fire.

It was so much water, you said.

You said she told you love stories. And other stories too.

You said there was never any telling what degrees of reality these stories bore.

Growing up I had collected so many stories and so many fragments of stories and fragments of things all revolving around her.

I drew all the stories from the little knowledge I had.

Sometimes I took one photo out of an album when it was in any way related to her.

I would take the photo and hide it and it always felt like I had just created the most exquisite secret.

Is it okay for me to tell you this?

Did you already know?

You must have known.

I like that her name is in our book.

I like that our book is still here.

I can still taste the thyme.

I can still see the ginkgo.

I didn't meet her when she was still alive, in the common meaning of the word, humanly alive.

But her name has a much familiar taste to it.

I remember this familiar taste being there from the very beginning. I don't think it's something I grew myself.

She feels like one of the closest partners in my life, like one of the most important people. Maybe this is strange.

But I am unwilling to consider strangeness a bad thing.

Last year I talked to someone about her ring.

We talked about the idea of belonging to a lineage.

I like this word.

I proudly belong to a lineage of strange women.

It must be one of the best lineages to belong to.

Are you still tasting the words?

We can always take a break.

Now I believe that our book will not disappear.

Not as long as we both imagine the ginkgo shapes. Not as long as we are both tasting the thyme.

YOU

I am awake now.

It is almost noon and I feel sad that the morning is over.

I enjoy the simpleness of mornings.

I get up and I stretch. This first encounter with my body every morning is a warm ritual, happening all by itself.

I like the taste of ritual. It is a comforting taste.

After the stretching I move my body. Then I shower.

I try to drink a lot of water in the morning.

That way I can make myself believe that it is easy to keep myself alive.

You just need enough water, I tell myself.

It's true. I need the water.

But I need other things too.

I need our book.

Thank you for making a book with me.

Do you think we can write my morning in our book?

It was a warm morning.

You were there the entire time.

Thank you for being there the entire time.

I talked to a student this morning.

I think they asked me about writing themselves.

I am carving out the spaces for them to write.

Do you think I am a teacher because you and him are teachers?

I do.

Thank you.

I think I love all the acts of teaching.

I do not think I enjoy the word 'teaching.'

After the moving, and the water and the shower I always wiggle myself into the shape of this new day.

Today this was my talk with the student.

After moving through the day for a small while, touching and tasting its edges and shapes, I get slightly dizzy from not having eaten yet.

The dizziness urges me to choose something to eat.

It is usually a hard decision to make because I don't enjoy eating in the morning.

But there is a lot of food in this house.

I like being here alone.

I like having it all to myself.

I like having it all to ourselves.

I think somewhere in our book we need to put a glass of orange juice.

And next to it we need to write a small cup of coffee.

The coffee is strong, and the cup is beige with thin blue lines. I found it when I was on a walk with a friend.

We need the glass of orange juice and the small cup of coffee. These are morning tastes.

I like how you have clouds in your cup for a few moments when pouring cold milk into hot coffee.

I do not like that the coffee is less hot then.

But I always choose wisely if there is coffee in my mornings. Because the coffee does not help with the dizziness.

I don't have time for coffee this morning. Because we are making our book.

Do you think I drink coffee because you drank coffee?

I do.

He drinks your coffee all by himself every morning. He is remarkable that way.

Thank you for teaching me.

Thank you for the book.

DOROTHEE

Is her name not the brightest name in the entire world?

Do you think she knows she is making this book too?

She might not know.

Did you know you are a writer?

Did it help when people told you?

This morning, I put on your earrings.

The ones you wore on the last of your human nights.

I heard you read a poem at dinner that evening. I like that so much.

And you wore the earrings with the pearls and the tiny dark blue stones.

She and I studied your jewelry.

She told me I could bring the earrings home with me.

Thank you, I said.

I don't think she knows she is making a book.

But she must be. All her colors are here.

All that yellow. All these dark shades of red.

I did not bring them. Did you?

I know.

They are distinctly her colors.

I think I will tell her about the book.

It makes sense that the three of us would make this book.

I will tell her soon.

YOU

This morning, I put on a new shirt I bought.

You liked it when I got new things. You would always inspect them thoroughly.

This shirt feels so soft against my skin. It makes me feel safe to be dressed in something this soft.

When I felt the safety and the softness, I went out to get the shirt in different colors.

All of them soft. All of them safe.

This one is light blue.

You often wore a shirt similar to this one, only it was light pink.

They would match so well. The colors, the shirts. We would match.

I can see it.

Maybe we should wear these shirts when we bring our book somewhere?

When we bring our book into its home, wherever that may be.

CANNIE

I like to tell people the story to this name.

When people get very close to me it is bound to happen that they overhear me being called 'Cannie' some time.

I always enjoy it when they ask – with a look of warm confusion,

What did they just call you?

Cannie, I say.

It is a family nickname, I say.

I smile.

There is a story to it, I say.

This conversation is one the most regular and one the most sweet rhythms to my life.

Do you want to hear the story, I ask them then, smiling.

They always say yes.

I always tell them the story.

They always smile.

There are so many smiles in that story.

Do you think that is because you are there in the story?

I do.

This conversation is a choreography I dance with everyone I love.

When I was little, I tell them.

When I was little and had just started speaking, I tried to say my name.

I tried to say 'Cara-Julie.'

For someone who just started speaking, I tell them, it is a very difficult name to say.

What I ended up saying was 'Jannie.'

I would talk about this 'Jannie-person' (me!) constantly.

It made all of you wonder who I was referring to. You and him and her and my father.

Yes, you would say to me, whoever this may be, they can come with us.

Then, one day, I say when I tell the story, I was sitting with you on the couch.

I would explain to you once more about 'Jannie.' About how it was *my name*.

You did not understand.

Until very suddenly you did understand!

Until very suddenly I could say 'Cannie'!

You jumped up.

You gathered him and her and my father.

I have figured it out, you said.

She is saying her name, you said.

I was.

I was saying my name.

Thank you.

People smile at me after the story.

I smile back at them.

It is one of my best stories.

I am still 'Cannie' now, I tell them.

Thank you for my names.

YOU

I have only very little time right now.

But I really want to keep making our book.

What do you think it means to make a book?

Because I don't think I know.

I just want a place for us.

I want us making a thing that is not only a thing.

I want to pour myself somewhere.

I was at your house today.

I just got back.

Everything is different and everything is the same all at once.

He talks about your picture a lot.

He always uses the same sentence when talking about your picture.

When I look at her picture, he says.

And the sentence stops there.

It is a sentence that is both always and never complete.

He was not talkative today.

But he had assembled an interesting collection of different rotten foods.

We cleared out the collection after gathering it on the counter.

Then I found noodles and frozen spinach and I made us lunch.

I put thyme in the spinach.

NOAH

Now I'm back home again.

I am making another thyme tea.

It's good his name is in our book.

I believe he had this house all to himself once. Like I do now.

The house we both grew up in.

It seems like an entirely different house, when there is no one here and you know no one is coming, too.

I wonder what it felt like to him.

Do you think inhabiting the house alone re-interpreted it for him too?

What did you think of the house?

I am not sure I know.

Do you think we can put two entire houses in our book?

The one we grew up in.

And the house of you and him. The house the three of us lived in for a small and sweet while.

I like making our book so much.

I don't want to stop.

But also, I want the book.

Because a book that has been made is probably a different kind of entity than a book that is in its making.

I am excited what the book *is* at that point in time, where we will say,

We have made a book.

The two of us.

The three of us.

And so many more.

We put two entire houses in that book, we could say, come see.

The book is a house.

Thank you for the book.

Thank you for the house.

YOU

I just unpacked my groceries.

I found thyme in the fridge!

This must mean everything.

ALWAYS YOU

There are no ginkgo leaves in the driveway today.

But when I step into the hallway a small wooden ginkgo leaf greets me even before the ginkgo drawing does.

I'm glad.

I am still wearing your earrings.

He didn't talk much today. But sometimes he does.

He talks about your teaching.

He talks about your writing.

He talks about your breakfast.

I don't know what we can put in the end of our book.

It seems clear how one makes a book.

But it is not clear how one ends a book.

It is also not so clear to me what we are making when we are making a book.

Do you know?

Do you think I ask this many questions because of you?

Maybe we can put some more ginkgo leaves in our book.

Can I tell you about the first time I visited the house after you died?

Yes, this is a story of ginkgo leaves.

And I taste the thyme in my tea while writing the ginkgo leaves into our book.

I remember little detail about this day.

I remember cooking what I believe was lunch.

I remember sitting with him.

I remember holding hands.

We hold hands very often these days.

I remember the crying.

I remember I wanted to walk through the entire house. Slowly. Before leaving for that day.

I walked every room.

As I said before, everything is vastly different and vastly the same all at once.

I think I gave water to your flowers that day.

I would do this in the days that followed, too.

I spent the longest time in your bedroom.

There was a stain of your blood on the curtain.

I knew about the stain.

I did not know it was so big.

I did not know it would hurt so much to look at it.

After I had caught my breath, I drew open every closet door one by one.

I looked at your clothing.

I studied your clothing.

Every time I open one of those doors, it smells like you so much.

I make my way further upstairs.

As always, it is coldest in the room you always did laundry in.

I move myself through the space.

I look at the clothing.

I look back at the shapes of a life paused.

I want to turn around and leave.

But somehow my gaze stumbles upwards.

There are raindrops on the window.

There are ginkgo leaves on the window.

Thank you.

ACKNOWLEDGMENTS

This book was never written or made alone. I am on the quest to find some words for all the forms of being-in-relation that are interwoven with this book. You are invited to stay with me on this journey. If you know me, please stay to find your name in one form or another. If you do not know me, please make this part into the place where you feel through all your ways of finding life and expression as a being-in-relation.

My honest and deep gratitude is with Fuente Fountain Books. Even in my warmest dreams I could have never imagined such a warm and kind space for me and my ginkgo leaves, for me and this book. Thank you, Michael Favala Goldman, for your kind editing, for your appreciation for these words and your wisdom and magic in editing. Thank you, Lynette Yetter, for one of the loveliest Zoom calls of my life, for a cover that moved me into many joyful tears and thank you for knowing everything this book was and needed from the very beginning. I have such deep appreciation.

Dear Paloma, I am not sure I have any words for what you are to me, but I do want to try and find some. My life has never been the same since you entered it and my writing has never been the same either. Thank you for making the music I need, for reading me and writing me, and for always knowing everything. Thank you.

My very deep gratitude is with all my family members. Thank you for raising me, for encouraging me, for loving me. Thank you for carrying the chapters of this book with your names. I give a special thanks to my grandmother, who is the true maker of this book. Thank you so much for your writing, Grandma. Thank you, Mom, for being a writer and for making me one too. Thank you, Grandpa, for being the beautifully and amazingly wonderful creature you are. Thank you for being so deeply intelligent in all the ways they don't teach us in schools. Thank you, Christine, for teaching me for my entire life how there is love and connection beyond boundaries of what we call life and of what we call death. Thank you for giving me your ring so I could write!

Thank you to Christoph Brunner for a PhD supervision that moves through my life as a golden thread of encouragement and of feeling seen; thank you for understanding my being-in-relation-with-writing so amazingly well.

Thank you to Kira, to Nici, to Jette, to Franci, to Noah, to Miriam, and to Steph for the depth of your listening, of your encouragement, and of your acceptance for me.

Thank you, Chiara, for our conversation on lineage. It still moves me now.

Thank you to the wonderful writers who composed the praise-prose for this book. I appreciate your words deeply.

Thank you to Erin Manning for your many writings. They encouraged me in forming loving relations with my ways of autistic perception and my more-than-human tendencies. This book would not exist without this encouragement I found in your work.

Thank you to Julietta Singh, to Maggie Nelson, and to Clarice Lispector. This book would not have existed without your writings.

Thank you, Hooki, my more-than-human love, for teaching me your unique languaging each and every day. I love you.

Thank you to the lake I sat at when discovering Fuente Fountain Books. Thank you to my windmill, my special place of rest.

Thank you to all my books and all my houses.

Thank you to everyone reading. Thank you to everyone writing.

ABOUT THE AUTHOR

Cara-Julie Kather is a feminist theorist and writer. She is committed to languaging in all its facets, to her own autistic perceptions and her many body-minds. She believes in writing as a mode of living and a way of togetherness.

Her writings include academic as well literary modes and all the inbetweens and beyonds to those categories. Some of her works can be found in *transcript*, *Polylog* and the *Journal of Ecohumanism*. She is currently doing a PhD on decolonial-feminist perspectives on mathematics. She has been and will be living in many different places together with her more-than human companion Hook: the most recent one being Hamburg, Germany, and the most lovely one being the home of her grandparents.

ABOUT FUENTE FOUNTAIN BOOKS

FUENTE FOUNTAIN BOOKS is an independent publisher based in Portland, Oregon, with distribution worldwide by Ingram. We specialize in progressive multicultural feminist books. We're proud that our first title, the bilingual book *Adela Zamudio: Selected Poetry & Prose*, translated from the Spanish by Lynette Yetter, was a finalist for the prestigious PEN Award for Poetry in Translation.

Fuente Fountain Books—where good ideas bubble up.

www.FuenteFountainBooks.com